ABC and 123

Coloring, counting and tracing

For Early Learners

Vachala Argsakorn

Contents

1

Animal names from A- Z in alphabetical order and pictures!

Color Capital Letter: ABC
Color Small Letter: abc

Ant
a
a
A
Aa

Bat
b
b
B
Bb
B

Cat

Cc

Dog

Elephant
e
e
E
Ee

Fox

Ff

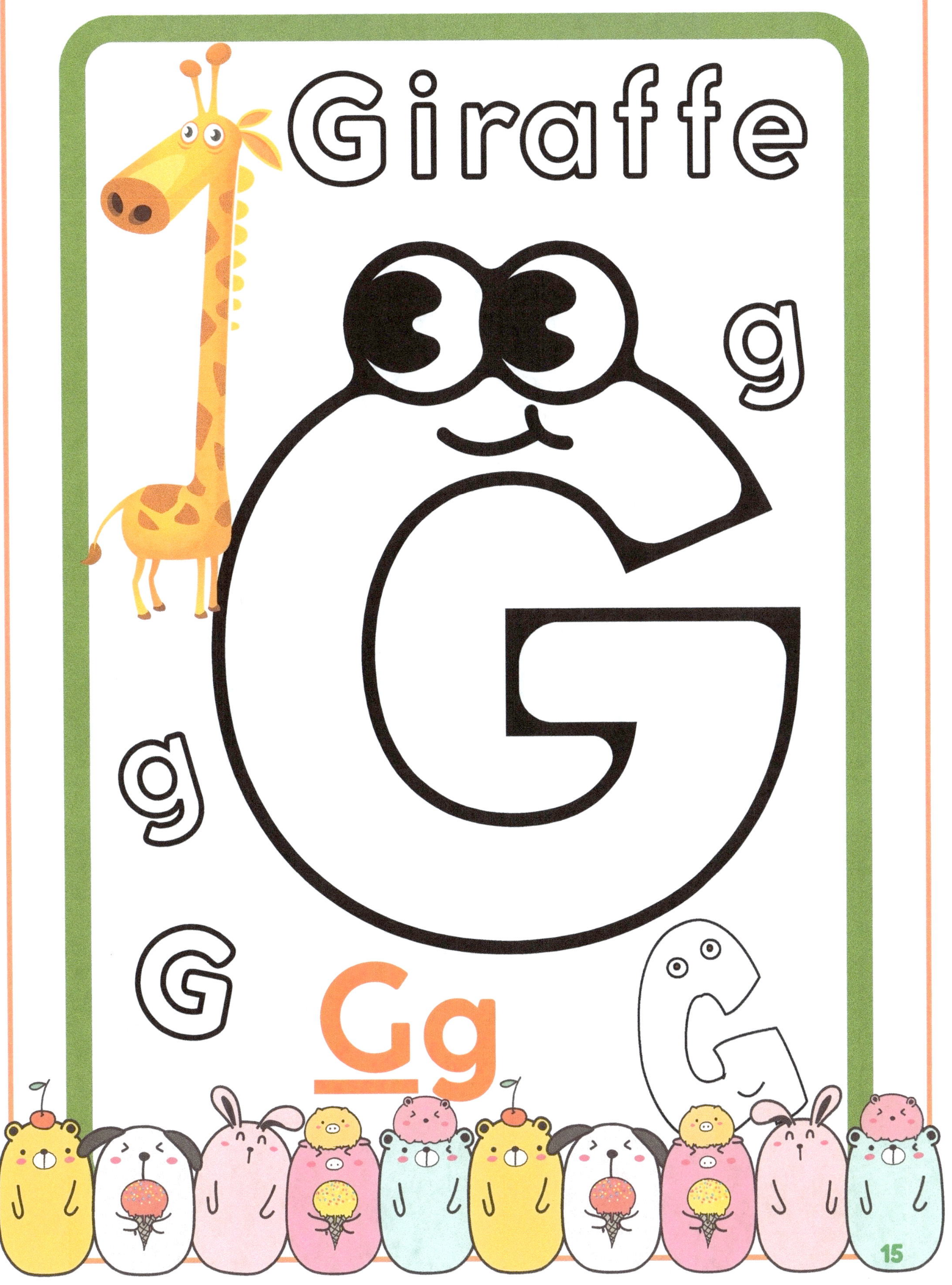
Giraffe
g
g
G
Gg
15

Hen

Iguana

Ii

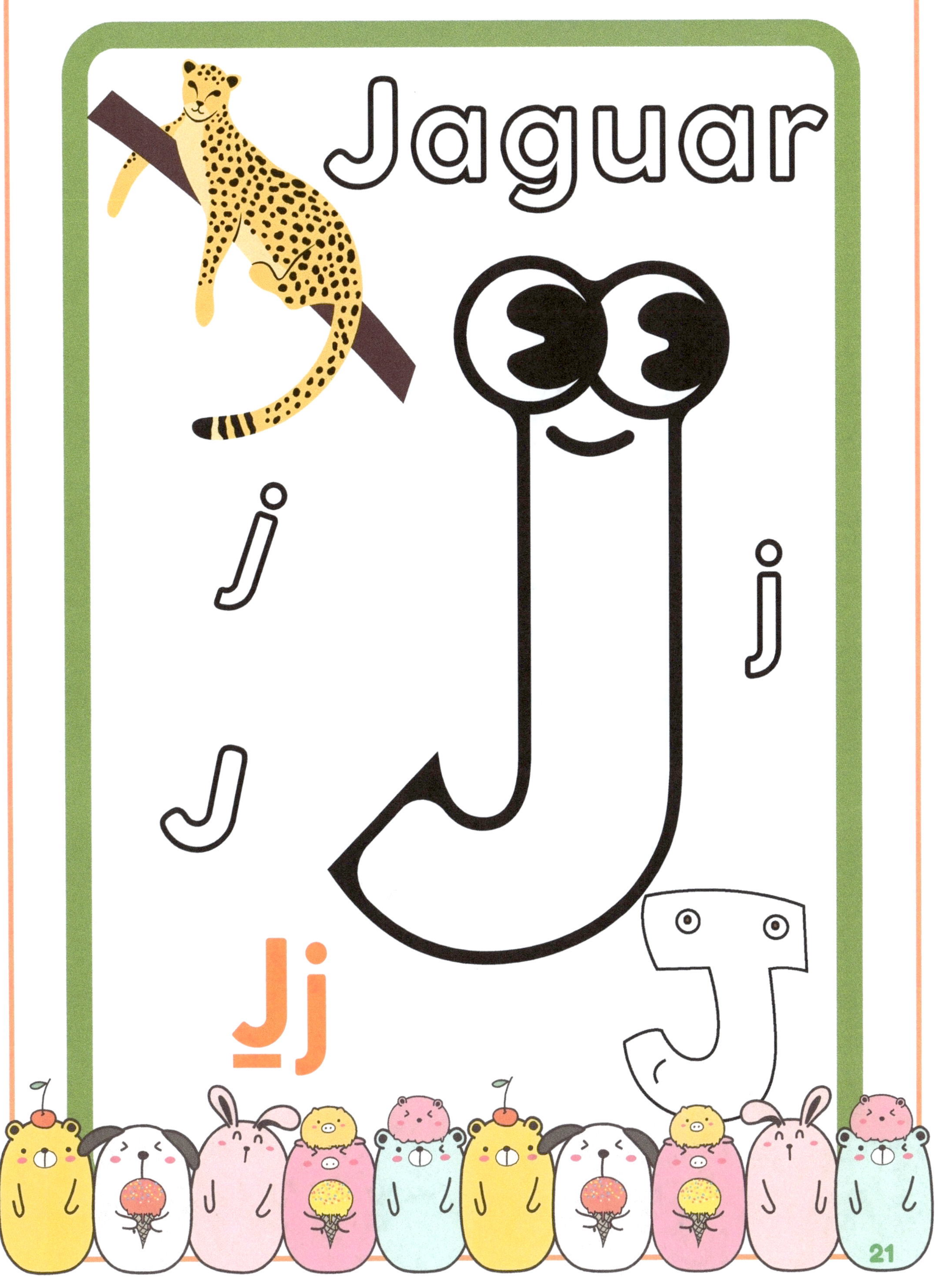

Jaguar
j
J
Jj

Koala

Kk

23

Lion
L
Ll
25

Monkey

Newt
n
N
N
Nn
N
29

Ox
Oo
31

Parrot

Quokka

Qq

Rabbit

Snake

S s

Ss

Turtle

Tt

Urchin

Vulture

45

Whale
W
w
w
Ww
47

X ray
fish
x
x
x
Xx
X

Yak

Zebra
Z
z
z
z
Zz
z

Number coloring, counting and tracing 1-10

Starting counting is a significant milestone in children's development.

By the age of 4, children usually can count up to 10 and/or beyond.

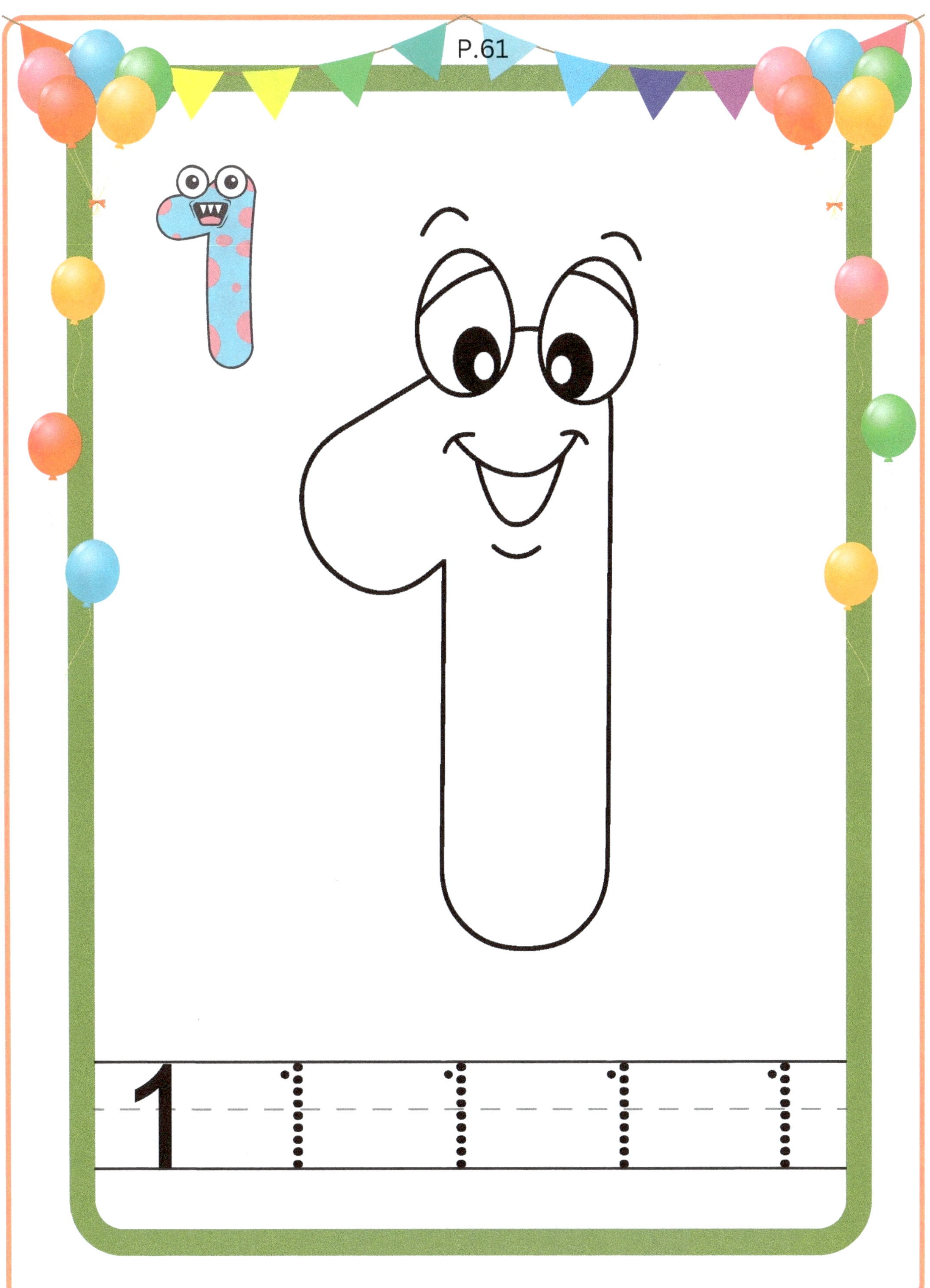

3 3 3
3
3 3 3 3

4

5
65

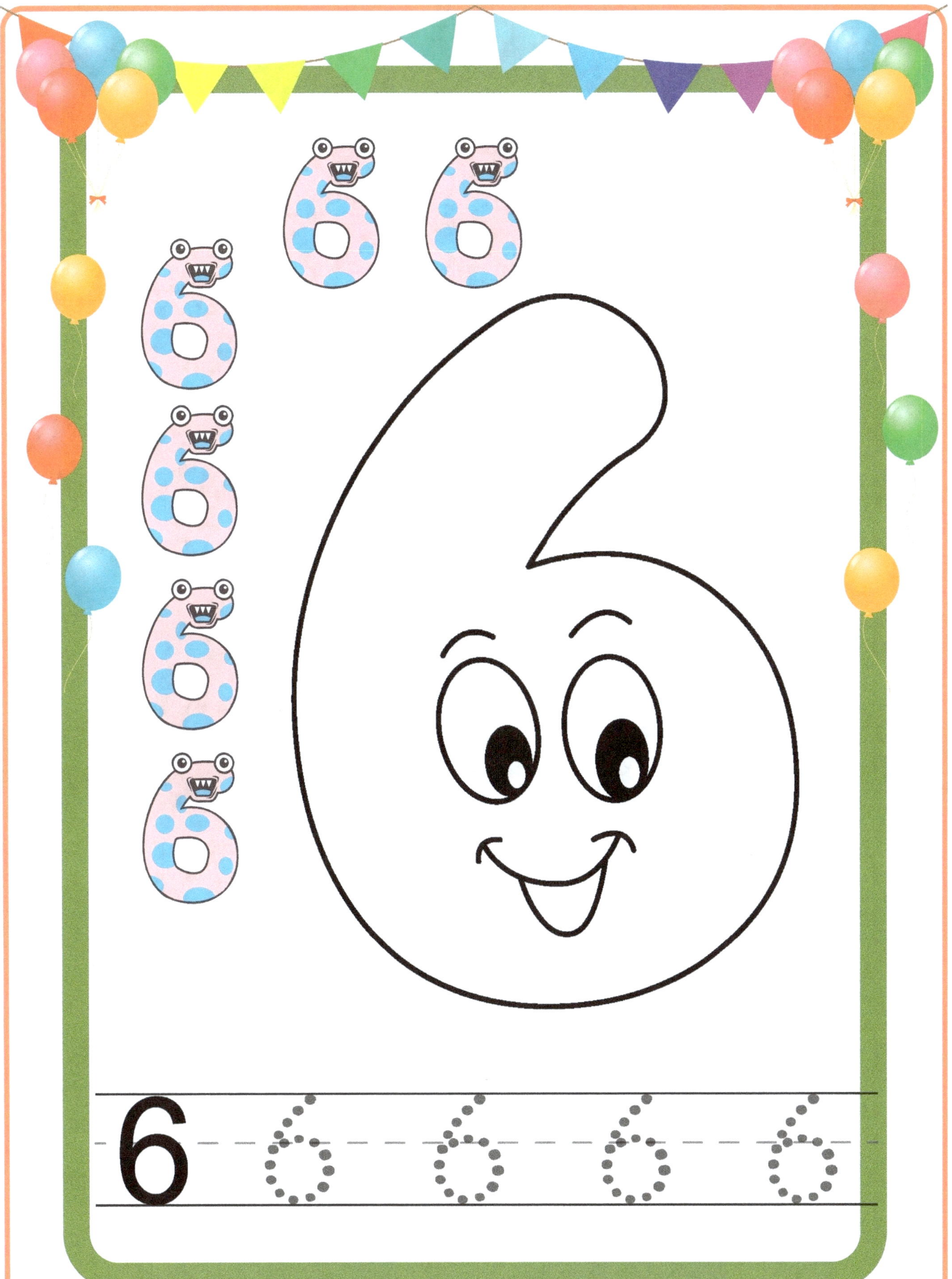
6
6 6 6 6
67

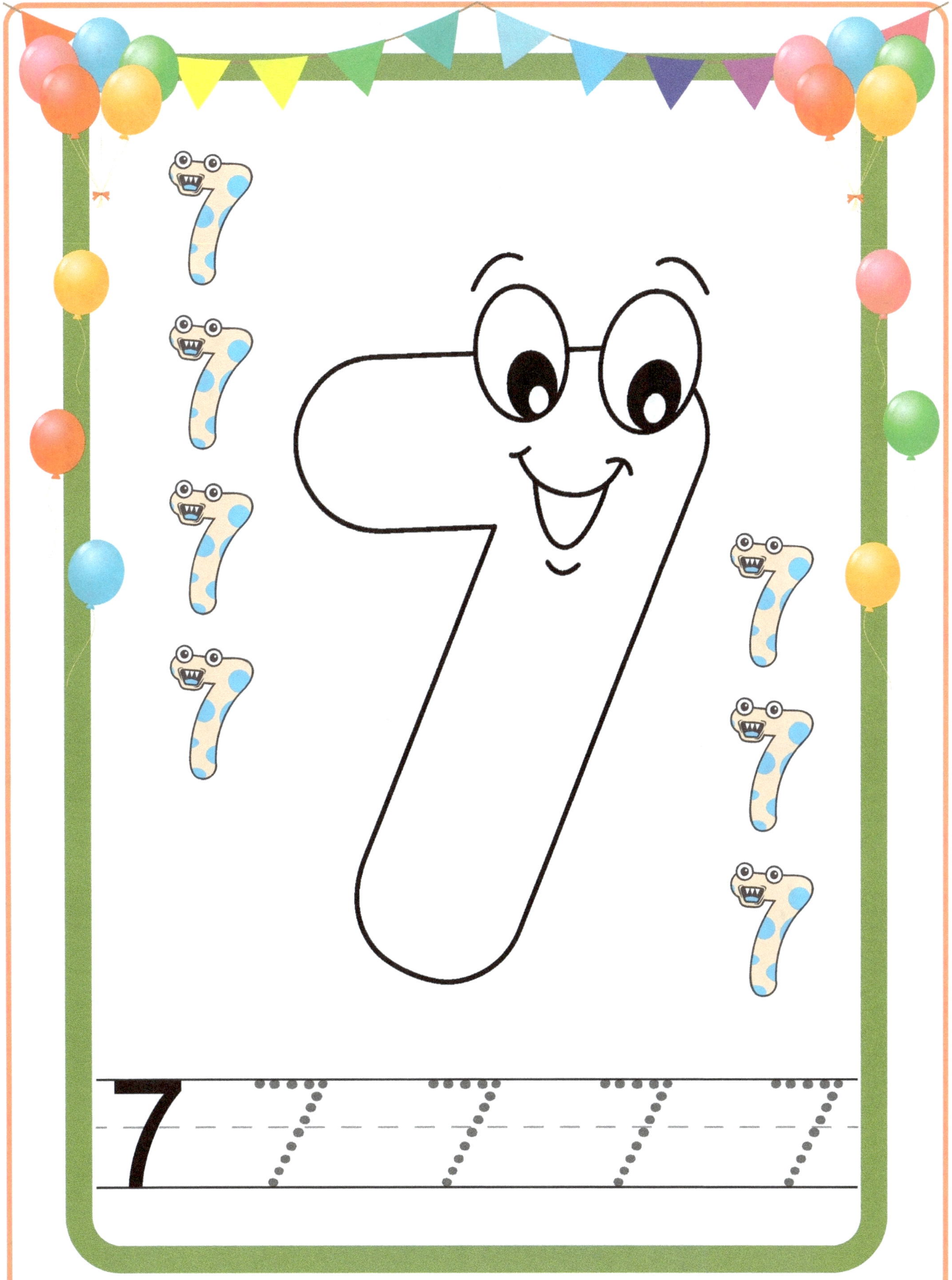

8

9

10
10

3

Coloring

ABC Alphabet letters and numbers

Fruit and Vegetable names in English and pictures!

The English Alphabet consists of 26 letters:

Letter Number	Letter		Letter Number	Letter
1	A		15	O
2	B		16	P
3	C		17	Q
4	D		18	R
5	E		19	S
6	F		20	T
7	G		21	U
8	H		22	V
9	I		23	W
10	J		24	X
11	K		25	Y
12	L		26	Z
13	M			
14	N			

23 from old English and 3 added later (J, U, W)

APPLE

BANANA

CHERRY

DRAGON FRUIT

EGGPLANT

FIG

G

GRAPE

H

HONEYDEW MELON

ICEBERG LETTUCE

JACKFRUIT

K

KIWI

L

LIME

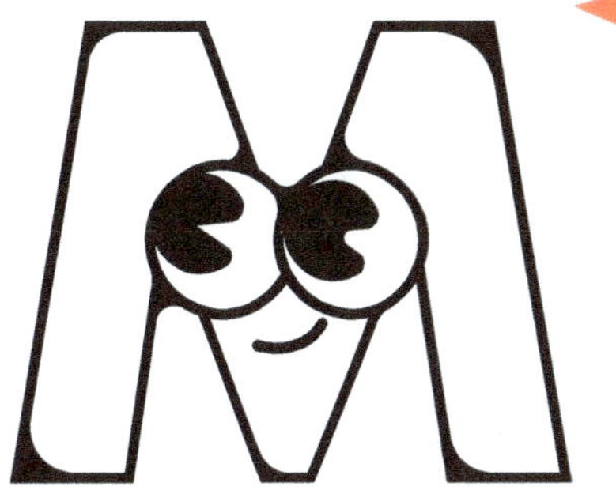

MANGOSTEEN

NECTARIND

ORANGE

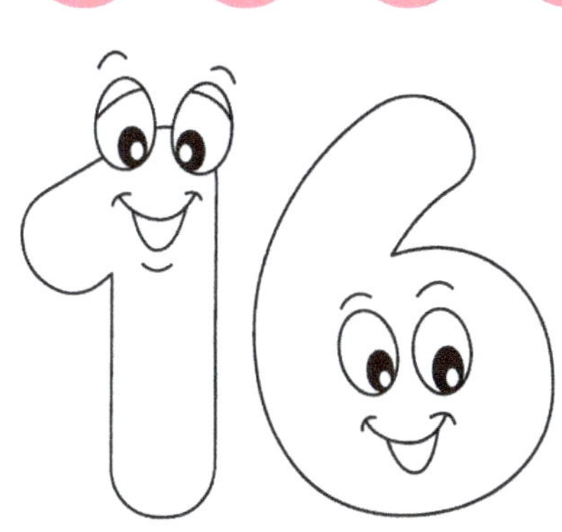

PINEAPPLE

QUINCE

RASBERRY

STRAWBERRY

TAMARIND

U
UGLI
V
VEGETABLE

23

W

WATERMELON

24

X

X-MAS TREE

25
Y
YUZU
26
Z
ZIZIPHUS

Wonderful !!!